EAT THIS!

365 Reasons to Stop Dieting

Mary McHugh

CHRONICLE BOOKS

SAN FRANCISCO

Library of Congress Cataloging-in-Publication Data:

McHugh, Mary.
    Eat this!: 365 reasons to stop dieting / Mary McHugh.
        p. cm.
    ISBN 0-8118-4158-8
    1. Reducing diets—Humor. I. Title.

    RM222.2.M4348 2004
    613.2'5'0207—dc21

                                            2003051508

Manufactured in China.

Eat This! 365 Reasons to <u>Stop</u> Dieting is
produced by becker&mayer!, Bellevue, Washington
www.beckermayer.com

Design: Todd Bates
Editorial: Adrienne Wiley
Production Coordination: Cindy Lashley

Distributed in Canada by Raincoast Books
9050 Shaughnessy Street
Vancouver, British Columbia V6P 6E5

10 9 8 7 6 5 4 3 2 1

Chronicle Books LLC
85 Second Street
San Francisco, California 94105

www.chroniclebooks.com

Diets don't work.

You're boring everyone
to death talking about it.

Marilyn Monroe
was a size 12.

4

Tap dancing is more fun
than dieting and burns
more calories.

5

One of the main rules
of dieting is "Never shop
when you're hungry."
A girl has to shop.

Zsa Zsa Gabor:

"At a certain age, dahling, you have to choose the body or the face."

(Choose the face.)

You'll gain it all back, plus at least 20 more pounds.

You're eating for two
(you and your inner child).

✦ ✦ ✦ ✦ ✦ ✦ ✦ ✦ ✦ ✦ ✦ ✦

How are you going to
belly dance if you don't
have a belly?

10

Chocolate fudge cake!

11

Making love burns 300
calories an hour.

• • • • • • • • • • • •

12

People have *died* taking
diet aids to increase
their metabolism.

Fat Girl Comeback #1:

They say TV adds 10 pounds,
so just by not being on TV,
you lose 10 pounds!

15

Children will love to
sit on your lap.

♦ ♦ ♦ ♦ ♦ ♦ ♦ ♦

16

Do you think Winston
Churchill ever said,
"I'm going on a diet?"
Of course not.
And he was still
pretty successful.

17

Fat-free cottage cheese tastes like old towels.

✳ ✳ ✳ ✳ ✳ ✳ ✳ ✳ ✳ ✳ ✳ ✳

18

Think about the thousands of workers in the plus-size garment industry whose jobs are on the line.

Everyone loves whales, and
they've got a whole layer
of blubber.

20

Gingerbread
with whipped cream.

• • • • • • • • • • • • •

21

You can finish all the
leftovers on your dieting
friends' plates.

22

Life is too short to deprive yourself of all that good food.

23

Diet drinks are like Chinese food: one hour later you're hungry again.

* * * * * * * * * * * *

24

When you went to your 20th high school reunion, the cheerleader who married the football captain was fatter than you were—and so was he.

25

Without the calcium in
all that cream cheese,
ice cream and butter, your
bones will get weak.

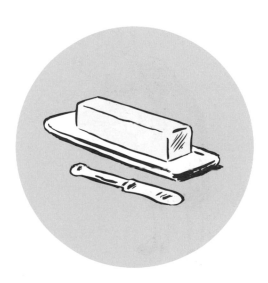

26

Your grandmother always says, "Eat, eat—you're too thin." And she's old, so she must be wise.

27

Life wasn't meant to be lived without pastries.

✦ ✦ ✦ ✦ ✦ ✦ ✦ ✦ ✦ ✦

28

You won't have to do without warm doughnuts and cider at the farm on a Sunday morning.

29

If a friend brings you a homemade loaf of cinnamon-raisin bread, what are you supposed to do? Throw it out?

Only 5 percent of the population has the genes to look like a model anyway.

Your friends cross the street to avoid you.

Sure, hypnosis helps you
diet, but your arm keeps
jerking up whenever you
hear the word "freezer."

❖ ❖ ❖ ❖ ❖ ❖ ❖ ❖ ❖ ❖ ❖

You can invest in some cozy
cotton sweatsuits, which
are incredibly comfortable
and also hide arm jiggles.

34

Early-bird dinners
of lamb chops and baked
potatoes with butter
and sour cream are a great
way to fuel up for an
evening on the town.

35

The very act of eating uses up 85 calories an hour.

* * * * * * * * * * *

36

You look glamorous in long, loose scarves, which also detract attention from any fat you might have hanging around.

37

You'll never need to diet if you look in the mirror every morning and say, "You are beautiful just the way you are and I like you a lot."

Santa Claus makes millions of children happy every Christmas, and he *never* diets.

39

Food tastes so good!

✦ ✦ ✦ ✦ ✦ ✦ ✦ ✦ ✦ ✦ ✦ ✦ ✦ ✦

40

If you play video games while your children are in school, you'll occupy both eating hands, and the adrenalin rush will burn some calories.

41

You're going on
vacation and you'll
lose 10 pounds thanks to
Montezuma's revenge.

42

Does anyone really think half a cup of *anything* is enough?

43

Rosie O'Donnell wouldn't make you laugh half as much if she were thin.

Ninety-five percent of all dieters never lose weight.

✦ ✦ ✦ ✦ ✦ ✦ ✦ ✦ ✦ ✦ ✦

You gave up smoking, and you're *hungry*.

46

Your mother won't look hurt anymore when you refuse her coconut cream pie.

47

Cooking for a dinner
party uses up 120 calories
an hour, which cancels
out all the tasting.

★ ★ ★ ★ ★ ★ ★ ★ ★ ★ ★ ★

48

Life is too short to go
without chocolate.

49

Fat Girl Comeback #2:

"Women who are too thin look so haggard, don't you think? Have you been getting enough sleep?"

50

You can wear flat-front
pants instead of
pleated pants and
look thin—and stylish.

• • • • • • • • • • •

51

You got rid of all your toxic
friends who made you want
to eat all the time.

52

Vacuum and dust
a little: 200 calories
an hour.

53

You've come to love your "before" photo.

◆ ◆ ◆ ◆ ◆ ◆ ◆ ◆ ◆

54

You just need a nap, not a diet. You won't be eating, and you'll get rid of some of the stress that makes you eat.

Romance novels
have started to feature
large, beautiful women
as heroines.

Banana bread with
lots of butter cries out,
"Stop dieting!"

57

Dieting brings
out your wrinkles.

58

Fifty thousand women who
went on a low-fat diet for
three years lost, on average,
just 2 pounds. So put some
cream cheese on that bagel!

59

Experts say to eat
peanut butter because
it fills you up.

✦✦✦✦✦✦✦✦✦✦✦

60

A plus-size modeling
agency wants *you*.

61

How many salads can you
eat in one lifetime?

Who can watch *An Affair to Remember* without a pint of butter pecan?

Even brushing your teeth uses up 30 calories a day (enough for a couple of cookies).

64

There's a reason that
it's not over until
the fat lady sings.

65

Too many young girls put
too much emphasis on
being thin. Show them
the error of their ways.

66

Your sex life is much
better than your skinny,
stressed-out cousin's.

• • • • • • • • • • •

67

Warm, rich mocha, full of
milk and whipped cream.

68

You were too thin
20 years ago anyway.

❖ ❖ ❖ ❖ ❖ ❖ ❖ ❖

69

It's not *you*—it's those
defective three-way
mirrors in department
store fitting rooms.

70

An order of bouillabaisse at a French restaurant *is* diet food—compared to the quiche.

71

Getting a makeover will make everyone think you lost weight, since you look so good.

• • • • • • • • • • •

72

There are lots of great things to do besides thinking about food and diets all the time.

73

If yoga uses up 200 calories an hour, doesn't stretching in bed use up about the same number?

74

You'll have a better chance of being hired as the pastry chef in a French restaurant.

Kate Moss has
put on weight—and she
looks much better.

Even fidgeting uses
up *some* calories.

77

Why would someone go to all
the trouble of honey roasting
individual nuts if we're not
supposed to eat each and
every one?

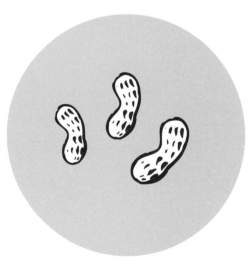

78

Ninety-five percent
of dieters who do lose
some weight end up
putting it back on.

◆ ◆ ◆ ◆ ◆ ◆ ◆ ◆ ◆

79

You discovered
procrastination caused
stress, which caused
overeating, so you no
longer put off trips
to the fridge.

80

Forget the raw carrots and cauliflower—you know what a really good onion dip cries out for.

★ ★ ★ ★ ★ ★ ★ ★ ★ ★ ★

81

You want to help all the people who've invested in fast-food stock, don't you?

Broadway *loves* fat people. The musical *Hairspray* celebrates them with "I'm a Big Girl Now" and "Big, Blonde, and Beautiful."

Whoever heard of
a jolly thin person?

You're sick of people
discriminating against
you because of your
weight, and you're
not going to take it
anymore, gosh darn it.

85

Hors d'oeuvres were invented to keep you from getting drunk. Load up on the bacon-wrapped scallops!

86

Shopping:
200 calories an hour.

✦ ✦ ✦ ✦ ✦ ✦ ✦ ✦ ✦ ✦ ✦ ✦

87

If you look at a mirror
from the front, not the side,
you'll notice your waist
comes in at the sides.
Thin girls don't have that.

88

If you don't eat a pizza,
how will you ever have
the energy to hike the
thousands of trails
out there?

You'll improve your chances of being cast as Queen Victoria in your community theater.

Jackie Gleason:
"The second day of a diet is always easier than the first. By the second day, you're off it."

91

Who would consider
Rubens' paintings
masterpieces if they were
full of skinny women?

92

If you go on a cabbage diet, no one will want to sit next to you.

◆ ◆ ◆ ◆ ◆ ◆ ◆ ◆ ◆ ◆ ◆

93

Veggies will never replace nachos as a satisfactory snack.

94

Fat Girl Comeback #3:

"Did you ever notice how grim thin women look? By the way, is everything okay with you?"

It's been shown that low-fat diets make people gain weight because they end up eating more calories.

* * * * * * * * * * * *

It's all the fast-food places' fault that you're fat anyway, so blame it on them and forget your diet.

97

The big game is boring
without a frosty, foamy
mug of beer and some
yummy munchies.

98

Who can eat movie popcorn without the butter?

Museums can be more fun
than eating—plus, you'll be
surrounded by all those
beautiful, round women in
sculptures and paintings.

Have you noticed how
great-looking plus-size
dresses are now?

101

When you're feeling sad, you need the comfort of rice pudding. Raw carrots just don't cut it.

102

Volunteer at a soup kitchen, and you'll realize how wasteful it is not to clear your plate.

103

Cleopatra looked more like Elizabeth Taylor looks now than when the movie was made in 1963. The Queen of the Nile was 5 feet tall and weighed 150 pounds.

104

Your husband is threatening to leave you if you don't stop snapping at him.

• • • • • • • • • • •

105

The Institute of Medicine at the National Academy of Science recommends more sugar and fat in our diets. Are you doing your part?

106

Dr. Atkins' diet allows you to eat lobster with butter, steak with béarnaise sauce, and bacon cheeseburgers—just add them to your other diet foods, and you'll be all set.

107

You can hire a cute
personal trainer and
concentrate on his buns
instead of sticky buns.

108

The saying is "Beauty is as beauty does," not "Beauty is as beauty weighs."

109

You'll be able to accept an invitation to join that club in France whose purpose is to taste the world's finest chocolate in candies and cakes.

110

You're cranky
when you diet.

◆ ◆ ◆ ◆ ◆ ◆ ◆ ◆

111

Women living in wealthy
neighborhoods are more
likely to be unhappy
with their bodies.
Your neighborhood isn't
wealthy enough to
warrant rice cakes!

112

The average woman is 5'4"
and weighs 140 pounds.
Don't you want to be
above average?

113

Skipping meals makes it
harder to lose weight.

114

Dieting makes
your breath
stinky.

115

Grilled cheese sandwiches
will bring back memories
of your childhood.

* * * * * * * * * * * *

116

Rake your lawn and burn
300 calories an hour = one
strawberry daiquiri.

117

Cruella De Vil kills puppies. It figures: she looks like she eats only lettuce leaves.

✦ ✦ ✦ ✦ ✦ ✦ ✦ ✦ ✦ ✦ ✦ ✦

118

You can tell people your extra weight is from the muscles you grew lifting weights at the gym.

119

Spaghetti and meatballs
is a must while watching
The Godfather.

Almond croissants.

• • • • • • • • • • • • •

Life is too short to make
a note of every calorie
you take in.

122

Reading the hardback edition of *Gone with the Wind* counts as a weight-lifting exercise.

123

Nutritionists say your daily meals should include at least two of the colors green, orange, purple, red and yellow. Strawberry shortcake, key lime pie, crème brûlée and a slice of cheesecake should do the job.

124

What's a summer picnic
without barbecued ribs
and corn on the cob
with lots of butter?

125

Double-dip mint chocolate ice cream cones take the sting out of back-to-school shopping.

◆ ◆ ◆ ◆ ◆ ◆ ◆ ◆ ◆ ◆ ◆

126

Don't you want to support your company's vending machines?

127

They say the way to achieve inner peace is to finish things you start. Today I finished a bag of potato chips, a chocolate pie, three sodas, a quart of ice cream and a small box of candy. I feel better already.

128

If breakfast is the most important meal of the day, doesn't it follow that fried eggs, bacon, a muffin and hot chocolate with whipped cream are more important than an egg-white omelet?

You can donate your
too-tight clothes to charity
and feel philanthropic.

You'll never have to let the
dessert trolley go by again.

Your **breasts** will be bigger.

Your breasts will be **bigger!**

133

Fat Girl Comeback #4:

"Yes, I have two kids! Did you say you were 38 and still childless?"

134

Italian and Brazilian
men will love the
way you look.

✦ ✦ ✦ ✦ ✦ ✦ ✦ ✦

135

Self-hypnosis is much
easier than dieting.
Just tell yourself you
won't be hungry every
night at 11.

If God meant for us to be thin, he wouldn't have given us hot fudge sundaes.

Washing the car uses up
300 calories an hour.

• • • • • • • • • • • • •

You can be a stand-in for
perky and plump Mrs. Claus
on Christmas.

139

Green apple-flavored
candy and red hots
improve your disposition.

140

Piano lessons will keep your hands so busy you won't have time to fill a bowl with ice cream.

* * * * * * * * * * *

141

Fifty percent of women are on a diet at any one time. Strike a blow for independence!

142

A long walk with a good friend is good; a big dessert with a good friend is better.

You'll discover how
much fun it is to be
a bad example.

Boston cream pie and
Sleepless in Seattle go
together like . . . bacon
and eggs.

145

You've just had a fantastic week and you deserve to eat anything you want.

★ ★ ★ ★ ★ ★ ★ ★ ★ ★ ★ ★

146

You've just had a horrible week and you deserve to eat anything you want.

How else will you
explain making
sarongs a staple of
your wardrobe?

✦ ✦ ✦ ✦ ✦ ✦ ✦ ✦ ✦ ✦ ✦ ✦

148

Scrooge is a good example
of a person who doesn't
eat enough.

149

Buttery soft pretzels and mugs of hot chocolate belong with ski holidays.

150

You're not fat—
you're womanly.

* * * * * * * * * * * *

151

Who needs to diet
when there are plenty of
two-minute exercises you
can do during commercials?

It's a *disorder* to look in the mirror and think you're fat when you look fine.

You figured out that you eat when you're happy—so what could be wrong with that?

You'll burn calories for two hours after lifting weights, so go buy some dumbbells, work out for five minutes, and chow down.

✦ ✦ ✦ ✦ ✦ ✦ ✦ ✦ ✦ ✦ ✦

Patti LaBelle:

"My stomach sticks out, I'm over 50, get used to it."

156

Diet programs make over
40 billion dollars a year.
Keep your share
for yourself.

157

Somebody has to eat all those bake-sale goodies.

★ ★ ★ ★ ★ ★ ★ ★ ★ ★ ★

158

Gwyneth Paltrow has to drink bancha twig tea to stay thin—yuck.

Most French people never diet, eat the best food in the world and are still thin.

✦ ✦ ✦ ✦ ✦ ✦ ✦ ✦ ✦ ✦ ✦

Making love in the afternoon makes you too hungry to diet.

161

Valentine's Day is no fun without a lacy box of chocolates.

162

Belgian waffles with real maple syrup.

• • • • • • • • • • •

163

You can join the Padded Lilies, a fat women's synchronized swimming troupe.

164

Your boyfriend
thinks you're beautiful.

★ ★ ★ ★ ★ ★ ★ ★ ★ ★ ★ ★ ★

165

Do you really believe it's
your *weight* stopping you
from wearing the clothes
worn on the runway?

Bicycle and burn 450 calories an hour = two pieces of coffeecake.

167

May 6: No Diet Day.

◆ ◆ ◆ ◆ ◆ ◆ ◆ ◆ ◆ ◆ ◆ ◆

168

Dancing along with Kevin Bacon in *Footloose* burns more calories than dieting.

169

Holidays are exempt from dieting . . . and every day's a holiday somewhere.

* * * * * * *

170

Dig out your old hula hoop and slim down your hips without giving up a morsel of food.

171

French pastries whisper,
"*Bon appetit.*"

✳ ✳ ✳ ✳ ✳ ✳ ✳ ✳ ✳ ✳ ✳ ✳

172

An order of mussels at an
Italian restaurant *is* diet
food—compared to the
fried mozzarella sticks.

173

Fat Girl Comeback #5:

"It was either keep smoking and die, or give it up and eat. I see you're still smoking."

174

When you're stressed out, a grapefruit just won't cut it.

★ ★ ★ ★ ★ ★ ★ ★ ★ ★ ★ ★

175

Nobody remembers
the musical genius
of *Slims* Domino.

176

Whoever heard of passing
a whole summer without
any hot dogs?

177

Flea markets are more fun with funnel cake.

◆ ◆ ◆ ◆ ◆ ◆ ◆ ◆ ◆ ◆

178

Even if you diet until you are the same weight you were when you were 21, your stomach will still stick out and your waist will still be thick. That's life.

Scale smashing is fun!

The pounds will melt away
when you swing dance to
anything by Glenn Miller.

The Wicked Witch in
The Wizard of Oz
might have been quite
nice if she had eaten
a little more.

182

You're the only one
who thinks you're fat.

• • • • • • • • • •

183

Would Aretha Franklin get
any "R-E-S-P-E-C-T" if
she was a twig?

184

Life is too short to spend
your time on a scale.

◆ ◆ ◆ ◆ ◆ ◆ ◆ ◆ ◆ ◆ ◆

185

Rich, dense,
delicious mud pie.

You can't knit and eat
at the same time or your
yarn will be all sticky.
So as long as you keep
churning out the sweaters,
you won't even be
able to overeat.

Dancing along to
an exercise video
is actually fun.

Picketing weight loss
clinics will make you
feel enlightened.

189

Eating cheese on crusty
French bread with your best
friend will help you solve all
your relationship problems.

190

Diets are expensive.

You can model in
fat fashion shows.

Walk off those pounds in
the city closest to you for
great people watching.

Plant some flowers,
pull some weeds and
burn 300 calories an hour.

✦ ✦ ✦ ✦ ✦ ✦ ✦ ✦ ✦ ✦ ✦

Take a yoga class for instant
serenity instead of eating
away your stress.

195

Jamie Lee Curtis says it takes 13 people working for three hours to get her to look skinny and toned. So either hire 13 people to get you ready every day, or relax and enjoy your life.

196

Meditation will never
lead you to the answer,
"*I should be thinner.*"
(Look at the Buddha!)

• • • • • • • • • • •

197

You're not fat,
you're lovable.

Water flushes the fat cells out of your body; there's water in Popsicles.

199

Clothes in your actual size
are always more comfy than
the ones you're trying to
squeeze into by dieting.

* * * * * * * * * * * *

200

The Zone, the latest diet
fad in Hollywood, will cost
you $5,000 a year.

201

Shrimp cocktail
has only 28 calories.

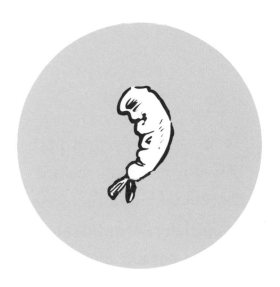

Forty percent of
women smokers smoke
to help them diet.

Food is an important part
of your personal reward
system when you've done
something sensational—
like get out of bed
in the morning.

204

Let's not even *think* about how Dracula stays thin.

205

You can simply stop
your craving for sweets
by pressing your thumb
or index finger firmly on
your opposite palm for 30
seconds, according
to acupressurist
Dr. Grigory Sadkhin.

Tasting is essential for good cooking.

207

There's only so much
time in one day for onerous
tasks; do you want to spend
it counting calories
or flossing?

208

Who cares if you can't still fit into your wedding dress? You're not going to wear it again, are you?

✦ ✦ ✦ ✦ ✦ ✦ ✦ ✦ ✦ ✦

209

Life is a banquet—why should you starve?

210

One size does *not* fit all.

• • • • • • • • • • •

211

Get a jogging stroller for your child, and enjoy those walks to the store while burning more calories than you'd diet away.

Fat Girl Comeback #6:

"Thanks for noticing my
pretty face! I was way
too thin before—about
your size, I think."

You can eat 15 delicious
little oyster crackers for a
snack, and they'll cost you
just 60 calories.

214

When you asked the Magic 8-Ball if you would lose weight on your latest diet, it said, *"All signs point to no."*

◆ ◆ ◆ ◆ ◆ ◆ ◆ ◆ ◆ ◆

215

Those subliminal message diet tapes keep you up at night.

216

What fun is Halloween
if you can't eat all the
leftover treats?

217

You'll meet fabulous people
in restaurants with delicious
fattening foods.

* * * * * * * * * * * *

218

With the money you save by
not going to a diet center,
you'll be able to buy a
beautiful new bike to
explore the back roads.

219

An order of fajitas at a Mexican restaurant *is* diet food—compared to the chimichangas.

220

Food is to pleasure as
diets are to deprivation.

* * * * * * * * * * * *

221

A whole piece of angel food
cake is only 124 calories.

222

Thin and cranky? Yeah . . .
like *that's* attractive!

◆ ◆ ◆ ◆ ◆ ◆ ◆ ◆ ◆ ◆ ◆ ◆ ◆

223

You can buy many more
CDs to play on your walks
every morning if you're not
forking over your money
to a diet program.

Gym class is way behind
you, and you'll never, ever
have to climb a rope again.

225

No matter what the ads say,
you cannot lose 10 pounds
in one weekend.

● ● ● ● ● ● ● ● ● ● ● ●

226

Isaac Mizrahi:
*"Emaciated frames
on women are out."*

227

Chocolate raises serotonin
levels in your brain, which
creates a natural euphoria.

228

The diet gurus keep saying,
"There are no bad foods."
Take them at their word.

✦ ✦ ✦ ✦ ✦ ✦ ✦ ✦ ✦ ✦

229

You'll have more money
to spend on a great-looking
bathing suit if you stop going
to a weight-loss program.

Pecan pralines.

Watch old Monty Python
skits and you'll laugh
yourself thin.

232

Attend an anger management class, and you'll no longer have to eat when you get mad at your spouse.

233

You can splurge on sexy exercise clothes for your aerobics class if you're not buying prepared food from a diet center.

234

You deserve those muffins,
cupcakes and yummy foods
because you're a good
person, and gosh darn it
people like you.

235

You can't lose weight
in just one lumpy
dumpy place.

• • • • • • • • • • •

236

Chewing gum when you get
the munchies will help you
lose 12 pounds a year
without dieting.

Dolly Parton eats lots of little meals the size of her fist every day instead of dieting, and *she* certainly looks healthy.

Puff pastry in all its wonderful forms.

239

All happy husbands of
plumpish wives will tell you,
"Thin women are nags."

✦ ✦ ✦ ✦ ✦ ✦ ✦ ✦ ✦ ✦ ✦

240

You *need* those
marshmallows when
you have PMS.

241

Look up "happy" in the dictionary—the word "thin" is never used in the definition.

242

Other women will
like you more.

• • • • • • • • • • •

243

Now that you have
a professional-quality
home entertainment system,
you'll need to keep the
pantry stocked with
movie theatre goodies.

No one thinks any less of Maya Angelou because she's bigger than a size 6.

Eggplant Parmesan.

Doughnuts have fewer calories than some of those high-fiber cereals they keep telling you to eat.

247

Eating with chopsticks is just as effective for losing weight as any diet.

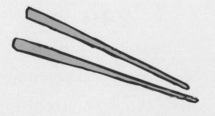

248

You can indulge in a facial, manicure and pedicure with the money you'll save.

◆ ◆ ◆ ◆ ◆ ◆ ◆ ◆ ◆ ◆ ◆

249

Some men and women are "chubby chasers." Find one of them.

250

Fat Girl Comeback #7:

"I'm negotiating with John Waters to be in one of his movies, and he asked me to put on a few pounds. Have you ever been in a movie?"

You don't need a diet, just more sleep. Sleep deprivation affects the hormones that control your eating, making you more apt to stuff yourself.

252

Life is no fun without homemade sugar cookies, slathered in frosting.

* * * * * * * * * * * *

253

A chocolate bar with almonds will give you the energy to whiz through your day.

254

You'll lose weight just by giving up nibbling while you fix the kids' dinners.

★ ★ ★ ★ ★ ★ ★ ★ ★ ★ ★ ★ ★

255

A handful of dark chocolate chips can help fight cardiovascular disease and stroke.

256

If you drink eight glasses of water a day instead of dieting, you won't have time to eat—you'll be in the bathroom all day.

257

Creamy, sugary cappuccinos
are much tastier than
black coffee.

✦ ✦ ✦ ✦ ✦ ✦ ✦ ✦ ✦ ✦

258

Chocolate syrup only
has 50 calories per
tablespoon, so put it on
everything—your cereal,
your raw carrots, your rice
cakes—or just pour it
directly into your mouth.

259

Drinking tea helps you lose 6 $\frac{1}{2}$ pounds a year, so fire up the kettle!

260

Extra weight is good for extra traction in winter driving conditions.

•   •   •   •   •   •   •   •   •   •   •   •

261

You don't want to be one of those mean, skinny women who change the subject when someone joins them at a restaurant.

262

An order of dumplings at a Chinese restaurant *is* diet food—compared to the spareribs.

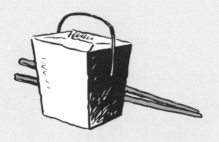

263

Life is too short
to give up snacking.

✦ ✦ ✦ ✦ ✦ ✦ ✦ ✦ ✦ ✦ ✦

264

The way to a man's heart is
through his stomach—and
you can't cook fettucine
Alfredo and make him
eat by himself.

If Kathy Bates can appear nude in the movies, you can certainly appear nude in your own bedroom.

◆ ◆ ◆ ◆ ◆ ◆ ◆ ◆ ◆ ◆ ◆

There are a lot of men out there who actually *prefer* women with a little meat on their bones.

If you're born with fat cells, why fight it?

You can completely cover a huge, rich scone in clotted cream.

269

If you're bored and tempted to eat, take a class in Vietnamese. At the very least, you'll know what you're really ordering next time you eat out.

270

You'll ruin holiday dinner for everyone if you don't have a second helping of stuffing.

Who but a nutritionist
would consider fat-free
cheeses fit to eat?

The word "snack" was
never intended to mean
vegetable sticks.

Cherry pie cures backaches
and headaches.

* * * * * * * * * * *

Five studies by the National
Institutes on Health failed
to prove that eating fat
caused heart disease.

275

Oprah Winfrey looks
fantastic fat or thin.

◆ ◆ ◆ ◆ ◆ ◆ ◆ ◆ ◆ ◆ ◆

276

Walking 15 minutes a day
will help you lose 12 pounds
a year; walking through the
"sale" aisle at your favorite
store counts double.

277

If you do ab-firming tummy tucks while driving, you can eat all the tiramisu you want.

· · · · · · · · · · · ·

278

Keep your hands busy making quilts for Christmas gifts and you won't have time to eat.

279

Your boss keeps leaving
oatmeal raisin cookies
on your desk as a hint,
because you're so crabby
on your diet.

Good sex makes you
crave chocolate.

◆ ◆ ◆ ◆ ◆ ◆ ◆ ◆ ◆ ◆ ◆

Walk an hour a day and
use up 280 calories =
two hot dogs.

282

Everyone says
you look tired.

283

Milkshakes are an important part of the "liquid diet."

* * * * * * * * * * * *

284

Strawberry shortcake is an absolute necessity when you're under stress—like when you break a fingernail.

285

Your stomach won't growl during the quiet parts of movies.

286

You won't eat out of loneliness anymore if you make a bunch of new friends at the pastry shop.

If you don't have enough
carbohydrates in your diet,
you can suffer from fatigue,
lack of energy, short-term
memory loss and vitamin
and mineral deficiencies.
Linguine with clam
sauce, anyone?

288

Eating is definitely an
aerobic exercise. Think
of all that chewing.

* * * * * * * * * * * *

289

Your brain is 70 percent fat.
Fatty food = brain food.

290

Your hair is falling out, your skin is flaking, and you have no energy. Eat! Eat!

• • • • • • • • • • •

291

If you invite 10 people who are all heftier than you over for a party, they'll tell you how thin you are.

292

Fat Girl Comeback #8:

"I gained back 15 pounds after my last diet, so that's what it was—my last diet. But you must be between diets."

You get rid of calories
every night by turning
your husband over when
he snores.

* * * * * * * * * * *

Deviled eggs
with lobster stuffing.

295

Your cat doesn't care if
you're fat or thin.

296

Personal trainers recommend eating a handful of macadamia nuts half an hour before running a marathon. Doesn't your life feel like a marathon?

• • • • • • • • • • •

297

Do you really *want* to look like Joan Rivers?

Your mother is fat. Your grandmother is fat. Your sister and brother are fat. All your cousins are fat. Do you really think you can beat those odds?

299

Luciano Pavarotti:
"The reason fat people are happy is that the nerves are well protected."

♦ ♦ ♦ ♦ ♦ ♦ ♦ ♦ ♦ ♦ ♦

300

Running your errands with a child on each hip burns enough calories for one day.

301

Whoever thought up the idea of "good" and "bad" foods clearly got their lists confused.

✳ ✳ ✳ ✳ ✳ ✳ ✳ ✳ ✳ ✳ ✳ ✳

302

If you're on a diet because your boyfriend said, "I fell in love with a thin woman," leave him and find a man who loves you just the way you are.

303

A ballet class burns 376 calories an hour.

★ ★ ★ ★ ★ ★ ★ ★ ★ ★ ★ ★

304

Donna Karan designs for larger sizes now.

305

Just moving from the couch to the refrigerator several times a day uses up calories.

People will say, "You have such a beautiful face," all the time.

✦ ✦ ✦ ✦ ✦ ✦ ✦ ✦ ✦ ✦ ✦

Your friends give wonderful dinner parties specializing in cream sauces.

308

Lots of doctors say, "As long as you feel fine, don't diet."

* * * * * * * * * * *

309

You realized you were spending 1 hour a day = 7 hours a week = 365 hours a year thinking about dieting, and now you have 15 extra days a year to enjoy yourself.

310

Twenty-five percent of the time, doctors cannot identify overweight patients simply by looking at them.

● ● ● ● ● ● ● ● ● ●

311

Fried clams.

312

The smell of peppermint is a natural energizer. Better candy canes than coffee.

313

You're healthy, you feel terrific and you love the way you look. End of story.

◆ ◆ ◆ ◆ ◆ ◆ ◆ ◆ ◆ ◆ ◆

314

Comfort food like macaroni and cheese makes you feel safe, happy and loved.

315

You can't afford to buy all new thin clothes.

* * * * * * * * * * * *

316

Go Latin. Learn the merengue, salsa, tango and mambo, and work off 353 calories in an hour—it'll be a lot more fun than dieting.

317

Ice skating and bowling are fun and keep you healthy and thin.

What if you won a lifetime supply of curly French fries and had to turn them down because you were on a diet?

You're *supposed* to eat more in the winter—it's one of nature's laws.

You can have an ice cream cake for your birthday and get your recommended dietary allowance of calcium.

321

Fish curbs your appetite better than other foods—so fish and chips is a diet aid.

322

They say you are what you eat. Do you want to be a bowl of bran flakes with skim milk?

★ ★ ★ ★ ★ ★ ★ ★ ★ ★ ★ ★ ★

323

Notice the smile on men's faces when they watch Jennifer Lopez walk away.

324

Fat Girl Comeback #9:

"It must be all the sex my husband and I have been having—makes us so hungry afterward."

325

When you were young, you were supposed to clean your plate because of the starving people in Africa. What's changed?

✦ ✦ ✦ ✦ ✦ ✦ ✦ ✦ ✦ ✦ ✦ ✦

326

Chocolate gives you the same feeling you have when you're in love.

327

Can you really enjoy Easter
without a chocolate bunny
and lots of jellybeans?

328

You're sick of making fried chicken and mashed potatoes for your husband and children and a stupid salad for yourself.

329

Would *My Little Skinny Greek Wedding* have been a blockbuster?

330

Comfort foods are comforting because they're full of good stuff, like butter and cream. What's comforting about skim milk?

331

The éclair.

★ ★ ★ ★ ★ ★ ★ ★ ★ ★ ★ ★

332

Play tennis for an hour and use up 450 calories = a bowl of ice cream.

A turkey burger will never, ever be as good as a real hamburger.

Soap operas often feature plus-size temptresses.

✦ ✦ ✦ ✦ ✦ ✦ ✦ ✦ ✦ ✦ ✦

Think of all the foods you've never tried! How can you start dieting now?

336

You need some fat in
your life to make your
complexion smooth
and luscious.

★ ★ ★ ★ ★ ★ ★ ★ ★ ★ ★ ★

337

Does anyone actually
like rice cakes?

338

Size 12 is the latest trend for women.

★ ★ ★ ★ ★ ★ ★ ★ ★ ★ ★

339

Fat floats, and what with that whitewater rafting trip approaching . . .

340

Get a dog instead and you'll walk off the weight.

Hang lots of pictures of
Renoir's naked fat ladies on
the walls of your bedroom
and bathroom, and you'll
feel slim as a supermodel.

✦ ✦ ✦ ✦ ✦ ✦ ✦ ✦ ✦ ✦ ✦ ✦

Run and burn 700
calories an hour =
1/3 lb. of prime rib.

343

You've yo-yo dieted so
much that you've run
out of string.

* * * * * * * * * * * *

344

Life is too short to
restrict your lunches
to celery sticks.

345

Beauty, health and fitness come in all sizes.

• • • • • • • • • •

346

What *is* tofu, anyway, and why would you deliberately choose to eat it?

347

Eating cheddar cheese
after a rich dessert can
reduce tooth decay
according to one
enlightened dental study.

So much chocolate,
so little time . . .

✦ ✦ ✦ ✦ ✦ ✦ ✦ ✦ ✦ ✦ ✦

You can buy a bunch of
romantic peasant blouses
that will make you look
gorgeous and feminine while
hiding your tummy.

350

Find a beach and watch the ocean roll in and your stress roll out, and you won't even feel like eating.

◆ ◆ ◆ ◆ ◆ ◆ ◆ ◆ ◆

351

You won't need to weigh yourself every morning and hate yourself because you gained an ounce.

352

If you must eliminate something from your regular diet, you can always choose broccoli.

Go to Hawaii, where the state attitude is "Hang loose," and you'll fit right in—literally.

✳ ✳ ✳ ✳ ✳ ✳ ✳ ✳ ✳ ✳ ✳ ✳

You can count carrot cake as a vegetable.

355

Julia Child isn't exactly skin and bones, but think of all the fun she had adding those pounds to her wonderful self.

356

You have food in your kitchen that's approaching its expiration date.

357

Fat Girl Comeback #10:

"Yes, I have put on a few pounds! Have you been ill?"

358

You have more important things to obsess about, like that annoying static cling.

✦ ✦ ✦ ✦ ✦ ✦ ✦ ✦ ✦

359

Follow Miss Piggy's diet advice: *"Never eat more than you can lift."*

360

Chocolate amaretto almond gelato. It must have been thought up by angels.

361

There are now women Sumo wrestlers, and you can be one if you put on a little weight.

Cereal is not an acceptable lunch food. Neither is tomato juice.

Snacking makes life worthwhile.

364

Christmas is gingerbread, Bouche de Noel, mashed potatoes and lots of stuffing in the turkey.